HEALDSBURG ALIVE!

Eight Sonoma County Writers Pay Homage to a Great Northern California Town

HEALDSBURG ALIVE!

Eight Sonoma County Writers Pay Homage to a Great Northern California Town

A HEALDSBURG LITERARY GUILD BOOK

McCaa Books • Santa Rosa

McCaa Books
1535 Farmers Lane #211
Santa Rosa, CA 95405-7535

Healdsburg Literary Guild
P. O. Box 1761
Healdsburg, CA 95448

ISBN 978-0-9838892-2-9

First published in 2012 by McCaa Books,
an imprint of McCaa Publications.

Printed in the United States of America
Set in Minion Pro

Cover photograph used courtesy of Barbara Bourne.
Image © Barbara Bourne Photography.

Cover design by Sharon Beckman.

www.mccaabooks.com

In Memoriam
Laurel Cook
Doug Stout

*This book is dedicated to Laurel and
Doug—the founders and guiding
lights in the creation and growth of
the Healdsburg Literary Guild.*

CONTENTS

Autumn

Preface

THE HEALDSBURG LITERARY GUILD is delighted to publish this new book, *Healdsburg Alive!—Eight Sonoma County Writers Pay Homage to a Great Northern California Town*. It follows a number of previous Guild publications, including *Present at the Creation* and three books entitled *A Day in the Life of Healdsburg*, in addition to several poetry chapbooks. This new book provided writers in the Healdsburg area with a four-session workshop in which to hone their writing skills along with an opportunity to publish their pieces.

Armando Garcia-Dávila, Healdsburg's 2002–2003 Literary Laureate, led the workshop. The price of admission included marvelous meals prepared by Armando.

The workshops met four times in 2010—once in each season. Armando opened sessions with a discussion of writing prompts, techniques, seeds, and subjects the participants might consider. Writers were then on their own for about three hours to wander Healdsburg and surrounding areas in Sonoma County, looking for inspiration for a story or a poem. Although the stated premise of the workshop was to write a piece that matched each season, writers followed whatever muse grabbed them and led their pens in preparation of a first draft. The group then reconvened and writers read their drafts. A lively discussion followed, offering each writer comments, ideas, and encouragement.

Armando then selected and edited pieces for the book. And *voila*, we have *Healdsburg Alive!*

We hope you enjoy it.

WINTER

Winter solitude—
In a world of one color
the sound of wind.
—Matsuo Basho

The River and the People
by Waights Taylor Jr.

Meandering out of the north, the Russian
River is enveloped in winter's grip:
steely dark waters, gray skies, bare trees,
and muddy banks filled with detritus
and flotsam from floods gone by.

The river wends around Fitch
Mountain ever seeking a path beneath
the dark skies to its destiny with the sea,
while daffodils, acacias, and mustard raise their
golden plumes to harken spring's coming.

He meanders under the river's two steel trestles—
a railroad bridge and a bridge for automobiles—
black holes for polluting fossil fuels.
Two fishermen stand on the railroad
bridge pier baiting their hooks.

The river and the mountain have so much
to tell—stories of the people who inhabited this land.
But first came the forces of nature:
the earthquakes, the glaciers, the floods;
shaping the land and its contours.

The first tribes came across the land bridge
from Asia's frozen tundra to the warm valleys.
The Pomo people shared the land with
the fish, fowl, and animals—none were
denied their dignity and right to survival.

The land gave the Pomo the acorns and seeds
for their pestles and the reeds for their baskets.
The river seemed to flow upstream, awash in bright
vermillion as instinctive salmon and steelhead
thrashed to their ancestral breeding grounds.

For thousands of moons, the Pomo lived
as one with the land until the strangers came.
First, the conquistadores came from the south
with their missions, ranchos, and a new god.
The Pomo's expulsion from the land had started.

Then from the west came the Cossacks
seeking new territories for furs, sea otters,
and trade. They also brought measles and
smallpox. An epidemic swept the people—
a tortured push from the land.

And finally, the allure of gold created a stampede
of Americans from the east—the Forty-Niners denuded
the mountains in their lust and then turned their
insatiable desire for land upon the Pomo, pushing
the people away by treachery, pestilence, and massacre.

The new people prospered, altering the land and
river with the trappings of the new society:
highways, bridges, and shopping centers.
The land was used for hops and prunes, and finally
grapes for wine to satiate Dionysus's minions.

The past, not to be forgotten, the Pomo people
returned with a bag of chips in one hand and
a bag of fool's gold in the other. The Pomo casino,
a temple to mammon, rises over the river
valley tempting all as Circe did Odysseus.

He yells to the fishermen, "Having any luck?"
"Nah," says the fisherman.
"Whatcha fishing for—steelhead?"
"Yeah."
He walks away thinking,
"Where did all the salmon and steelhead go?"

Surprise
by Chris Peasley

I wrote an essay about a gift I gave my mother one Christmas. When I asked what she wanted she always said, "Surprise me."

Took her up on her word. Donated five books in Spanish to my childrens' Immersion School. When I took her to the library to show her the books, she said, "I sure didn't know I wanted books I can't read."

I cried a little at her dismissal, but I laughed it off and after that she always said precisely what she wanted and I got it. Never asked her what she meant by her remark. I thought it was a great gift for someone with everything.

foreign answers
rolled up in paper
missed translation

Then she died. All the stories I wanted to hear she took with her. When they called with the news, they said my mother had died and I said, "My father you mean." "No your mother," said the nurse. I'm still surprised.

my father was ready
I was not
no more chances

A Winter Day in the Literary Life of Healdsburg
by Margo van Veen

Under a slate gray sky just outside Healdsburg City Hall
magnolias in bloom compete with the writers inside,
word lovers getting set for Third Sunday to have a ball
with open mic and guests on a magical ride.

> This is the last Salon held where a decade long
> those of the Guild kept going strong for the pleasure of all.

Poets already slowly are starting to trickle in.
Should we follow suit, or let the magnolias win?

> Pink blossom profusion creates the illusion
> of sensory confusion seducing the eye;
> north along Grove it roves to where
> across the street it gets to meet
> plum trees in bloom perfuming the air.

Under a gloomy sky by the mute Montessori school
the nose fairly glows inhaling that honeyed bouquet.
Even the ear is hearing bees buzz, though the air is cool,
chatter and laughter imagined of children at play.

> Now the eye doglegs back, follows the railroad track,
> opens the heart to urban art; by Oberti we start.

May Spirit Wall and Spheres offer respite in bold concrete,
may it graze evermore, Tedrick's fabulous horse.
Under a wintry sky, spirits bright, we re-cross Grove Street
senses now primed for literature at the source.

> City Hall's last Salon is such a special one
> featuring Healdsburg's own new laureate, Stefanie Freele.

Third Sunday's parting gift to its venue is such a deal:
Poems and prose; it's fun, and it's free, and it's Freele!
Under a Healdsburg sky, may it thrive for the commonweal.
Third Sunday Salon, for word lovers it's the real deal.

At the Lake in the Season of Loss
by Armando Garcia-Dávila

I RODE DOWN WEST DRY CREEK ROAD on my way to the man-made lake and passed a dead deer, later a raccoon and then a skunk; "road kill," such a cold and undignified description of the remains of God's creatures. Maybe it is not the best day to have come out here. It's grey with a chilled wind blowing. It's the first time that I have ever heard water lapping the shoreline of the lake. Weather report called for possible showers, but like a person who ages gracefully, there is always a beauty about Lake Sonoma.

Water is feminine; life emerged from the sea. Madrones, oaks, California bays, manzanitas don't have the stressed look of late summer but are beginning to show the effects of the first winter rains with moisture in their trunks, branches, and leaves.

"Lake drownings this year 0," read the sign at the entry. The year has scarcely begun, still plenty of time. I've heard or read about drownings in the Press Democrat over the years, though I have never personally known anyone who drowned here.

My daughter lost a classmate to the lake when she was in sixth grade; a handsome, athletic and popular boy with a Spanish surname. "Yes," she answered when I asked her if she cried at the memorial service. "Most of the girls did," she said. "He was lying in the casket, but it didn't look like him. His hands that held a prayer book were so still, and they looked funny like they weren't made of skin but something cold and hard and he was so still. I wanted him to open his eyes and sit up and tell us that he was going to be in class tomorrow – but he didn't. His mother had to be held up when she tried to walk out of the church after the service." Seems unfair for my daughter to have gone through that experience at such a tender age; death shouldn't be real until one's bones start to ache.

A turkey vulture glides from one side of the lake to the other. It caught the scent of death, and then makes its way to the carrion I passed. It is serving its function in keeping the world from the hazards of rotting flesh. Something like an ancient god of the Aztecs whose task it was to eat the sins of the world.

The grey of the clouds matches the water of Lake Sonoma. She is a beautiful and formidable body of water even in the dead of winter.

Jimtown Store: February
by Mona Mechling

THE CHRISTMAS HOLIDAYS HAVE PASSED; my best friend and I are breaking the fast that is imposed on our friendship because of family commitments in winter. Driving on Highway 128 east out of Healdsburg I can't help but smile as the blooming mustard comes into view. The days of rain in late January have subsided, blessing us with a sunny weekend as February peeks out boldly.

I arrive first and seize the opportunity to bask on the sunny front steps of Jimtown Store. I want Jana to hurry and get here so we can eat our lunch. I've started looking at the menu board, and my mouth is watering at the thought of buttermilk apple slaw alongside my half of the turkey chipotle sandwich on crusty baguette.

As Jana arrives I start spilling news about Danny and Tiffany, my sailor son and his bride. Tiffany drove her ancient car across country along Interstate 10 to Florida with two sisters and the dog to be there while Danny spends two months at his training school for the job he will do in the U. S. Navy. This is their only chance at newly wedded bliss just before his deployment that will come soon. As proud mom and now mother-in-law, I carry the emotions of their journey as badges on my heart.

The offering of this unexpected spring-like day makes me shed the melancholy that has paced me in January. With our food ordered, we give a glance to the mercantile part of Jimtown Store as we look around to secure our table. Shopping is a treat left for after lunch.

The quilt we see in the other room past our steaming cups of tea is amazing. That it's an antique was more than apparent but not due to shabbiness, quite the opposite. Earth tones with brilliant thread running through it as a contrast, made with a loving hand. We would have to wander by the quilt holder and check it out more closely.

Approaching it I catch something in a glimpse from the corner of my eye. Was that a trick of the winter afternoon light or did I see a face in the fabric? Right then Jana nudges me, and we both gasp at what we think we must be seeing. A shiver goes down my spine and not because I feel a chill. We decide we'll make some inquiries about the quilt before we leave.

Returning our attention to our food, we share the savory flavors of our lunch. Our conversation turns back to the quilt but also to the interesting menu selections here. What fun it would be to peek into the brain of proprietress Carrie Brown. Peanut butter and bacon together on a sandwich, such an odd combo. Mmm, mini cornmeal empanadas with choice of dipping sauces, now that's more to my liking to try next visit.

We've been coming so long we don't actually remember what brought us here the first time. It quickly became a welcomed habit that was hard to break with the excellent fare, warm atmosphere, and central location. With a friendship that is over thirty-five years old, we create escapes like the Jimtown Store visits to help retain our mutual sanity.

As our precious time together draws to an end, I look back at the bright yellow building surrounded by vineyards and realize that I'm leaving a part of me here in these worn walls joining the others in the ongoing story of Jimtown Store.

A Winter Day in the Plaza
by Dave Mechling

I sit in the plaza
Under steely grey skies
Expecting rain
As barren trees
Keep watch over me.
A fountain in the plaza
Gently bubbles away
I toss a coin
And wish for warmer days

Couples bundled up
Against the cold
Scurry in and out
A mother watches
As her children run about
Playing tag

The distant din of traffic
Pierces the quiet
The metal bench
Is cold and hard,
Making my bones ache

Yet here I stay
Mesmerized in quiet reflection
Of the year's past events
The war
My son's pending deployment
The lagging economy
The uncertainty
Of what lies ahead
All weigh heavily
On my mind
This dreary winter day

Stalking the Muse: Luther Burbank was Right!
by Margo van Veen

S O MANY PLACES FOR INSPIRATION! I head for the Russian River. Dave is already chatting with a woman in her front yard. I roll down my window and offer him a ride. He declines, prefers to stalk the muse on foot. I roll up my window. It won't. Now what? Near the Freeway I find Fincher's Auto Service. The big man behind the counter, Mr. Fincher I presume, is assisting an older couple. He acknowledges my presence with a friendly nod and smile.

I survey my surroundings. It is a fairly large place with a high ceiling and the requisite coffee table strewn with newspapers and magazines. The ubiquitous overhead television shows glamorous ladies with fruited hats à la Carmen Miranda advertizing some Pacific island.

Awards, diplomas and testimonials grace a low partition next to the counter. In the far corner near the back wall I notice a light colored sofa set. Its upholstery in yellow and reseda green reminds me of Italian dinnerware. The overhead TV turns a blind eye. But wait. I see possibilities. Take away the low table, add a few chairs and a microphone and it could be the new home for the Healdsburg Third Sunday Salon! Would Mr. Fincher be open to poetry and prose? I wonder. The kennel placed in the middle of the low partition tells me he is a dog lover.

Finally Mr. Fincher walks out with his customers. They say good-bye and the woman hugs him as if on impulse. I love him already, this big man with the friendly face and short white beard. In less than ten minutes he fixes my problem and I'm on my way. Almost twelve thirty. Only two and a half hours left to find inspiration in or around Healdsburg on this gray winter day with rain in the forecast.

Driving South on Old Redwood Highway, a small country road really, I find myself pondering the absence of sequoia sempervirens. Where have all the redwoods gone? Under the darkening sky the landscape's colors grow duller. The few bicyclists here and there add the only bright note so far. With their bobbing heads, pointy helmets, and multi-colored garb they look like exotic birds. But the mustard fields in bloom are stunning even without the sun. They remind me of the bulb fields in Holland where in my youth I was a tour guide, and of the lavender fields in the South of France where I spent a whole summer once.

Next stop, East Side Road Regional Park with its gravel pit lakes. A father tries to explain the honor system to his young son. He narrows it down to "No pay, no park" and lets the boy feed the hungry yellow mailbox. From the way it avidly gobbles up the day-use-fee envelope you can tell the whole park system is starving.

The boy sees me reading the entrance sign. "We are going fishing," he volunteers.

"Is that right! Lucky you. Have you fished here before?"

He nods. "Last time I caught a fish, but it was too small. We had to throw it back," he adds matter-of-factly with just the tiniest hint of regret.

Instant flashback: My brother and I, about the boy's age, sit on the side of one of the many drainage ditches in Rotterdam, fishing for pike or anything else that will bite—bread and freshly dug worms for bait.

I wish father and son luck and move on. Although the park offers excellent recreational possibilities, such as hiking, biking, birding, and fishing, I won't be saving the parks today.

Next, a stop at Shone Farm, that well-hidden gem and show case of the Santa Rosa JC Agricultural Department. It's the largest junior college farm in the nation. They even make their own wine. Turns out the place is closed on weekends. A llama shows me how it chews, lower mandible moving from right to extreme left and back under a flapping, hare-like, split lip.

It is now quarter to one. Here comes the sun! At once the mustard fields on my left start to brighten and glow, their vivid yellow echoed by a huge acacia in full bloom on my right. I can see the Wohler Bridge now and the Russian River below; but I don't stop, fond memories of bicycle-rides-past spurring me on across the one-lane bridge.

Wineries were at the bottom of my morning list of topics, but when I notice the Porter Creek Vineyards sign, I cannot resist. It is those bike rides my husband and I used to organize for out-of-town friends in the eighties. From Westside Road we would loop through the Russian River Valley to Healdsburg and via Eastside Road back to the Wohler Bridge, stopping at some wineries along the way. Porter Creek Vineyards was not one of them, I'm sure. I'm intrigued.

The tiny tasting room with its redwood beams and picture window is both quaint and charming. The jovial host is explaining to a young couple how last year's grape-killing frosts make this year's harvest that much more abundant and flavorful. The man pouring the wine prides himself on being a foremost pinotlogist and touts the virtues of their organic wines, all from locally grown grapes. A busload of tasters piles in; time to continue my literary quest.

Under a newly overcast sky, I walk by an aviary with colorful Australian parakeets. In the middle of a tree-lined meadow a tiny planked platform seems to float on clover; an ideal spot for jotting down my musings to the murmur of a babbling brook. "Oh, perish the cliché!" I mutter, about to cross out that old bromide. But then Armando's gentle voice echoes in my head: "Don't edit. Just write. Let it flow." In spite of the workshop leader's whispered admonitions, I can't help wondering. How *does* one write about a piece of paradise that *defies description*, or is *too beautiful for words*? Oh, there we go again! I dutifully ignore the staid turns of phrase. Now and then little birds chirp and chatter. Slowly it dawns on me. Why try to reinvent the wheel? Luther Burbank was right! He said it best: *"The Redwood Empire is the chosen spot of all the earth."*

It is getting colder now; the sun has not come back. Two thirty! Time flies when words flow like that proverbial babbling brook. For nostalgia's sake I make a last brief stop at the Hop Kiln Winery. Its building—now a historical landmark—dates from the BW era (the time before wine), when hops were grown for beer and dried in its three kilns. It alone is worth the visit. However, this is no longer the unassuming little winery it was in the time of our bike rides of decades ago when Dr. Marty Griffin was the proud owner.

The new proprietors (2004) not only offer fine wines to taste, they also have a variety of upscale products to sample. Fancy mustards vie with interesting oils, organic preserves, and other snackable items for the attention of my palate. A few quick nibbles, merely to whet the appetite, careful not to spoil it, because in Healdsburg a feast is in the making.

Only ten minutes left to make it back by three for the second part of our Day in the Life of Healdsburg workshop; that's the one where all ten participants share and critique their results. Then part three: After the day's literary fare we will share the gourmet meal Armando, our modest moderator, bilingual poet, and chef extraordinaire, is preparing right now. Meanwhile, the other nine poets and writers like homing pigeons return to the workshop at the appointed time.

Oh, never mind cliché-overload, interior-rhimitis, and purple-prositis. Write! Write! Write! Write with abandon! Oh, the anticipatory titillation and salivation! I can almost feel the poetry, hear the prose, and smell the polenta already!

SPRING

First day of spring—
I keep thinking about
the end of autumn.

—Matsuo Basho

The Bamboo Pole and Me
By David Beckman

"MISTER! GET ME OUT OF HERE."

I was walking through the Healdsburg Plaza, and looked around for who had spoken, but no one was nearby.

"Right here!"

Next to me was a trashcan, and sticking out of it, a bamboo pole.

The voice said, "You've got to help me!"

I thought, okay, I've gone nuts. It was the pole talking, it's voice high-pitched and urgent.

"You're not crazy, dude," it said. "I'm alive and I can talk. Deal with it."

In spite of myself I took the pole out of the can. It was very light, maybe five feet long, one-third inch in diameter, light tan in color.

"Super," it said. "Your hand's a little cold, but who's complaining? Not me. Let's go."

Oh, great, I thought, now I'm about to talk to it. "Go where?" I whispered.

"The Flying Goat. You can have a coffee and I can get warm."

A huge part of me wanted to put the pole back in the trashcan and keep going. But some force overrode that impulse. It was cold and rainy, but the chill I felt came from within. I was about to enter some Twilight Zone of unreality. Holding the pole firmly, I headed toward Center Street, touching its bottom end lightly to the sidewalk.

"Hey," it said, "whadaya think I am, a walking stick? Just kidding, man. No problem, I'm happy to be on the move."

I -- we, arrived at the Flying Goat coffee shop at Center and Plaza Streets. It wasn't crowded inside, which was good. The fewer people who might witness my insanity the better.

"Go ahead," the pole said. "Get yourself a double latte mocha with espresso java cream and extra sugar, whatever. Nothing for me, I'm good."

My head was spinning, but I stayed cool. At the counter I ordered a soda, then, the pole still firmly in hand, headed for a table.

"Soda?" said the pole, sounding surprised. "Lemme see the bottle. Raspberry lemon Frizzy Lizzy? Weird, but okay. It's a free country -- not!" He kind of cackled.

I sat on the long bench that runs along the wall, placed him carefully against a table, opened the Frizzy Lizzy and took a swig. It was good...cold and sweet. Maybe it would settle my brain down.... give me some perspective on what was happening.

"Okay," I said. "Mr. Pole...do you have a name?"

"Nope, but I've got a life story. Wanna hear it?" Not waiting for an answer, he jumped in like he was on a mission. "I was born in a grove near Cloverdale. Earliest memory? I came poking up from the soil. Boom. I'm heeeere! A real little sprout. Had a mother, father and 42 brothers and sisters. Grew fast -- sucked nutrients and was happy. Put out little branches and leaves in a hurry. Fahgeddaboutit, as they say in New York.

"Only bad thing was this recurring nightmare of some kind of bear... black and white, big sucker -- in my dream it came into our grove, sat down, stripped off our branches and leaves, and ate like crazy. Had a name -- Panda. I dreamt that he ate my mom and about 20 of my sibs and most of my friends. That dream went on for a couple of months. Wow, dreams man, where do they come from?"

I shook my head and snuck a glance around the coffee shop. Maybe fifteen people were there by now. Could anyone overhear? Did I care? You bet I did.

"Anyway," the pole went on, "when I was four, the real nightmare started. Except this wasn't any dream. These guys, humans, came into our grove with harvesting knives. Bastards! Just did us like a lawnmower does a lawn. I mean, zip, zip! -- cut us at the ankles and laid us out. End of my happy youth.

"Next thing we're all in a truck, then offloaded into in a place off Healdsburg Avenue -- open air, full of plants, trellises, clay pots, you name it. Smell of eucalyptus and loam. We're put in a pile near the back. I'm thinking, where's Panda when I need him? I'd rather be dead than here.

"Next day some joker buys maybe a dozen of us and takes us home. The guy -- weird hat, iPod, earplugs, listening to Rosanne Cash. Love her sound. You like her?"

I whispered: "Me? Yeah."

"Cool. What she does with 'Sea of Heartbreak,' man, about fractures me."

For the first time, I realized I totally liked this bamboo pole. "Anyway," he went on, "iPod man takes four of us out to his garden where there's this young cypress tree. I mean a baby. So weak it can't hold its own branches up. The guy sticks us poles into the ground and ties its branches to us -- one branch to each of us so that we're like supporting the little runt.

"So, for, I dunno... a year and a half, we stand there in the garden. Cold, hot, wind, rain, dry, cold again, on and on. Only each other for company. No pay, no days off, no thanks. What is that? I ask you. I mean, where's my freakin' rights?

"Fast forward to yesterday. The iPod guy comes out, unties us from the tree, pulls us out of the ground. The cypress didn't need us anymore I guess, and neither did he. Anyone say 'Thank you'? No! So la-dee-da and kiss my skinny ass!

"It's all a blur after that. We're in the truck again -- me and the other poles, coming down Healdsburg Avenue, and you won't believe it -- we hit a bump and I fall out. Right out the back 'cause the idiot guy hadn't put up the tailgate. The total jackass! I land near a school, watch the truck and my friends tool on down the road and it's oh-my-God -- goodbye!

"Lying there, I was totally depressed. Like, I'm history. I'd have cried if I had tear ducts. Then some kid finds me, brings me to the Plaza, swats his buddies with me, and finally tosses me in the trashcan. Longest night of my life. I'd have prayed if I knew how. Then you come along this morning, and here we are."

I'd finished my soda. The Flying Goat was filling up. A family with two little boys was at the table next to us. One of the boys eyed the pole. I was nervous, sweating, because I read the pole's mind, what he'd say next.

He didn't waste a second. "So I got one question. What the hell are you gonna do with me?"

The Month of Mary
by Armando Garcia-Dávila

I T'S MID AFTERNOON at the downtown Plaza. Most of the Mexican men hoping for a day's work have long gone. A young Mexican family passes my bench. The papa says, *"quedate aquí conmigo hijo,"* (stay here with me son) taking his little boy's hand to keep him from running into the street. His wife carries an infant wrapped in a blanket. It's as perfect a spring day in Healdsburg as I have experienced. It is warm but not hot, a profoundly deep blue heaven overhead; a slight breeze blows from the west.

May; it's the month of roses and the Virgin Mary. I didn't like it that Ma had the family get on our knees once a month after dinner to pray the rosary. We recited the Glory Be's, the Our Father's and Hail Mary's over and over until we mumbled them trance-like as mantras. My older sister leading the prayers raced through before the "Dick Van Dyke Show." In May, we had to pray the rosary every night in honor of Mary the teenage girl impregnated by God who would give birth to His Son.

It is said that she is the only person to never have sinned. She was pure and every woman is to emulate her. I suppose that is one reason that sex is considered a duty rather than carnal pleasure among the women in our family. My brothers, sisters and I are a testament that Ma did her duty at least seven times.

I wonder if this young Mexican family passing me are Catholic and worship the same ancient Jewish deity as our family, or have they been swept up in the evangelical tsunami engulfing the Mexican culture over the last few decades?

When Ma and her sisters attended mass in Mexico they wore black lace mantillas to cover their hair lest somebody think them vain or they exact a righteous castigation from the good priest.

I walk to the west end of the plaza toward a bench occupied by two middle aged Mexican men engaged in casual conversation. I make eye contact with one.

"Buenas," I say with a smile. Simply saying, "Buenas," is enough among Mexicans. It is like greeting someone in the culture of the *Norte Americanos* by saying, "mornin."

"Buenas," answers the man with a smile. His name turns out to be Serafín, his partner is Edgar. Both are in good spirits as they had found work earlier and have returned to the Plaza to do what Mexicans do so well; socialize. Serafín got work with one of his regular customers who needed help getting her yard ready for a garden party. He and Edgar have returned

"*aver si nos toca otro pescado aunque sea chico,*" (to see if we might snag one more fish even if it's a small one).

In short order we know where each other's families have originated. "Your father is from Sinaloa?" Edgar says. "They say that the women from there are pretty tough and '*hablen recio*' (speak roughly)" he says with a laugh. "I was there once and a woman hit on me, and right in front of my wife!"

I miss this, I think to myself, being around people who are so at ease in the world, people who don't die of stress and are as comfortable talking with a stranger as with family. I think that both would be an ideal CIA mole though I don't think Serafín or Edgar would be interested in a job involving deception. I notice that each wears a thin gold chain around his neck. Between Serafín's shirt buttons I am able to see enough of a gold medal to know that it has the image of Mexico's patron saint. Our Lady of Guadalupe, the apparition of the Virgin Mary who appeared to a humble Indian man named Juan Diego.

It's a safe guess that these two are traditionalists still worshiping the same deities as my mother. It would not surprise me if they and their families are praying the rosary on their knees every night this month.

Spring in the Plaza
by Dave Mechling

The bronze boy scout
Folded flag in hand
Welcomes me
As I enter
The plaza

Free from winter's
Cold embrace
Where once barren trees
Pop with new life
In a palette of greens
Camellias in full bloom
Keep off the grass signs
Guard young shoots

An old golden lab
Enjoys a cool drink
From the plaza's fountain
Bicycle riders
Wearing a rainbow
Of colors
Pause to socialize
And have a quick snack
A young couple
Tiny tot in tow
Ohh and ahh
Pointing to a butterfly
As it floats past

Feeling the warm sun
On my face
A gentle breeze
Tickles my nose
With the scent
Of roses and
Orange blossoms

The grand band shell
Full of young lovers
Sitting arm in arm
Lost in their own world
Spring with its promise
Of new life
Has finally arrived

Reach Out
by Chris Peasley

The helicopter flies high above.
The emblem on the body
almost too faint to read.
A Reach Helicopter,
sent to medical
emergencies and rescues.

Headed up the Russian River to
assist with a drowning.
Paramedics are pounding
on the victim's chest.

They transport the man to
the helicopter that is
perched on the road, the chopper
blades kicking up a fury of dust.
They struggle, working in tandem
to move the victim.

No one is optimistic
but they keep up the CPR.
When they reach the hospital
the doctor calls time of death: 15:33.

Blue Moon
By Waights Taylor Jr.

GODDAMN IT'S HOT. I can't stop tossing and turning. Jesus, only late May and our first heat wave is hitting in full force—triple digits for three days and no sign of a let up.

I look at the clock for the umpteenth time. One o'clock and almost bright as day—a full moon, a blue moon, brightens the sky with the luminance of a small sun and fills the bedroom with its golden glow.

I flip a few more times, surprised my wife isn't awake and annoyed with me. Finally, I give up, get up, and roam the house like a lost soul unsure and anxious about what to do or where to turn.

I get dressed—jeans, a T-shirt, and sandals—jump in my car and take off not knowing where I am going. I drive around town for a while, and then decide to head for the coast—the ocean and the headlands will be awash in the moon's bright rays. Not paying any attention, I suddenly find the car driving north as if it has a mind of its own—past Wikiup and Windsor, and towards Healdsburg.

I drive past the Healdsburg Plaza, and as if drawn by a guiding hand, I find myself at the entrance to the town's old cemetery. The gate is locked. I park. It is quiet, and no one is about. I easily climb over the fence and walk among the tombstones and grave markers bathed in the iridescent moon glow.

I walk up the hill to the now defunct tipsy fountain. I sit on the edge of the fountain and marvel at the trees surrounding me—oaks, bays, redwoods, laurels—their trunks playing in the lunar shadows and their leaves aglow with a golden sheen. The nighttime creatures add their harmonious sounds to this surrealistic scene: frogs are the bassos and tenors, the grasshoppers and cicadas the timpanists, the small birds the altos, and an owl seems the concertmaster with his occasional hoot.

I sit quietly, observing and listening—I don't know how long, almost in a meditative state—when I notice a movement out of the corner of my eye in the trees to my right. I turn—nothing, then I see a wispy shape slowly moving from tree to tree towards me.

I freeze, transfixed as the cloud-like apparition nears. Then, not believing what I see, the translucent shape slowly evolves into a man: a man of about forty to fifty years old, medium height and build, a beard, and well-dressed in nineteenth-century clothing complete with a gold watch fob across his vest.

As he walks the last few feet towards me, he says in a deep, melodic, baritone voice, "Good evening sir. My name's Heald, Harmon Heald."

Breathing rapidly, unsure, and yes, afraid, I stammer, "I----Go----Good evening----I----."

"Don't worry sir, I'm not going to harm you."

"What—what are you and who are you?"

"I told you, I'm Harmon Heald."

"But you're dead. I know you're buried near here. Are you a ghost?"

"We'd rather be called benign spirits, if you please."

"I'm sorry, no offense intended, but I've never experienced anything like this. You said 'we.' Are there others like you about?"

"Oh yes, this is a special night—this extra full moon always brings many of us out.—What's your name?"

"Waights, Waights Taylor."

"An unusual name."

"It's Welsh."

"Well, Welsh Waights, may I sit down and talk for a while?"

"Yeah sure. My god, what's going on?"

"What you see has been going on since time immemorial, Waights."

"But I've never seen anyone like you or heard of anyone who really has, although lots of people make some wild claims."

"It's this night, Waights. For reasons neither you nor I can understand, you've been chosen to be here and to see."

"Harmon, -- may I call you Harmon?"

"Of course."

"Harmon, I'm terribly confused—I don't know what to think right now."

"What do you believe?"

"I'm, or was, an atheist. I believe human life on earth ends in all manner and forms when you die. Yet, unless my eyes deceive me, I'm wrong. Am I wrong?"

"I'm not a prophet. I have no answers for you. Each of us has to seek our own truth. But we are here."

"Where are the rest of you, Harmon? I don't see anyone but you."

"Maybe that's all you're allowed to see. The others are about in the trees, and below the hill. Some even elect to remain at home."

"Home is your grave site?"

"Of course, where else do you think it might be?"

"I'm not thinking clearly, Harmon. Can we change the subject for a moment?"

"Uncomfortable talking about your beliefs?"

"Yeah, I guess so."

"What do you want to talk about, Waights?"

"Well, let's see. Do you realize what a prosperous and well known place the city of Healdsburg, your namesake, has become?"

"I've heard stories over the years about the many changes in the town."

"Oh, it's great. The Plaza is still the center of town surrounded by numerous stores, restaurants, and wine tasting rooms. Have you gone to see the town?"

"NO! It's not allowed. It's against the rules."

"Rules? You have rules?"

"Of course. You think we live like savages?"

"No, not savages, but spooks."

"Please Waights."

"Sorry, this is just so strange. What are the rules?"

"There are many. But to your question about visiting town: we are not allowed to leave the cemetery."

"What happens if you do?"

"It's not written down, but years ago on a night like this, we experienced an example of the consequences. Old Sam Bloomfield just decided he'd had enough with the cemetery and said he was going into town. We begged him not to do it, but he insisted. Most of us were gathered on this hill watching as he drifted toward the cemetery gate. When his form crossed above the gate into the 'other' side, there was a bright explosion that quickly dissipated into the air. We never saw Sam again, and no one ever tried to leave again."

"Then you're really trapped here?"

"That's a bit dramatic. We are free to wander and socialize within the confines of the cemetery."

"Is it like this in all cemeteries?"

"How would I know? I only know I can't leave here. If there are others like us in other cemeteries, I assume they have the same rules."

"I'm sorry Harmon, but this is really weird. You are almost like vampires, and ghosts and goblins coming out only at night."

"Oh Waights, Waights, don't—you've been reading too much Edgar Allen Poe."

"Well, I think you'll agree that to a non-believer like myself, this is hard to comprehend and accept."

"Maybe it's all a dream."

"I know it's not a dream. I've been wide awake all night."

"Well then, what is it?"

"I got it! It's a practical joke—you and some other jokesters dress in period costumes and do this occasionally just to frighten and upset a person."

Harmon breaks into a long, loud laugh that is equal parts a deep-throated humorous roar and an eerie howl.

As his laughter subsides, we sit looking at one another saying nothing. I realize that it is deadly quiet—absolutely no sounds—the creatures have ceased their melody. The silence is so noticeable that its lack is like a sound unto itself—it is deafening.

Finally, the owl emits a single hoot, and his mates erupt into a cacophonous screech. A second hoot from the owl restores the players to their melodious harmony.

I look incredulously at Harmon, and say, "My god, are you in control of everything in this cemetery?"

He laughs again, more a chuckle, and says, "No, I only live here along with all the others. But it does seem Mr. Owl may be in control.—Waights, that's the second or third time you've invoked god's name tonight. Do you or don't you believe in god?"

"No I don't. I've never seen or read anything that convinces me there is a god figure. I mean, look at the history of man and religions—there's nothing in our behavior or in what might be considered god's behavior to convince me otherwise. —Although, maybe I'll believe in the devil after tonight."

"Believe in nothing or whoever you want to. It will change nothing. We are here for the rest of eternity."

"Harmon, I guess it's the thought of spending eternity in heaven or hell, or in this cemetery like you that really frightens me. 'Of all the base passions, fear is the most accursed.'"

"Ah, Shakespeare. How about: 'What fools these mortals be.' You humans spend your hurried, short lifetimes fearing the unknown after death. You create facades to shield that fear. Believers create a façade of faith, and paint their hopes of an afterlife in a golden frame called Nirvana, Valhalla, or Heaven where eternal pleasures await. Agnostics hide behind a façade of indecision, hedging their bet on either side of the coin. And atheists, like you, use a façade of decisiveness to absolve yourselves of facing eternity by refusing to believe anything."

"You may not be a prophet, but you've certainly become the philosopher."

"Unlike humans, time is now our friend, and we use it to think on many things."

"Is that it, just thinking? Don't you get lonesome? What about sex?"

"SEX! Is that all you human males think about?"

"No—well, maybe—yeah, most of the time. But I do have moments when I think about my work and intellectual pursuits."

"Waights, you really need a change."

"Is this the change I have to look forward to?"

"You see me. You experience this place tonight. You have to decide, but more likely, you'll have to wait and see."

"How will I ever explain this night to any one?"

"Don't even try. They won't believe you—they'll think you're mad.—Waights, there is one thing I can tell you."

"Yes?"

Harmon suddenly looks to the southeast and says, "I'll have to be leaving soon."

"Why?"

"The first glimmer of dawn is in the sky. Sunrise is coming soon. Another rule: we must be in our homes before the sun rises."

"What happens if you're not?"

"I don't know. Probably the same thing that happened to Sam."

I turn and look quickly at the southeastern sky. As I turn back, I say, "Harmon, what were you going to tell—"

All the creatures are silent.

Villanelle for Sam
by Margo van Veen

You don't waste precious time with wondering why
Disease should strike these old and weary bones
The flame of life once lit one day must die

Your candle dwindles; this you won't deny
Remembering fondly places where it shone
You don't waste precious time with wondering why

The cancer struck, thus forcing you to try
Retirement, oh rest for weary bones
The flame of life once lit one day must die

Why you? your saddened friends and kinfolk cry
Your voice betrays an urgent undertone:
Let's not waste precious time with wondering why!

You've lived life to the full and by and by
Eternal truth has seeped into the bone;
The flame of life once lit one day must die

Heroic measures waived, you bravely sigh
While nurturing the seeds of peace you've sown
You don't waste precious time with wondering why
The flame of life once lit one day must die

Jimtown Store: May
by Mona Mechling

THIS WARM SATURDAY IN MAY finds me driving to the Jimtown Store on highway 128. The vineyards are alive with bright orange California poppies and the roadside is bordered by wild violet sweet pea. The first strawberries of the season have come out reminding me of my son Danny who always wants strawberry shortcake for his birthday dessert.

This visit is a Mother's Day treat for my best friend Jana and me. We share much as mothers along with being best friends. Our only children, boys, are very similar in personality and close in age and the angst I feel over Danny leaving for duty in the Navy she is now experiencing first hand as her son prepares to leave for college in a few months.

This afternoon Jimtown has been transformed from sleepy country store into a rest stop on what appears to be a cycling tour through the county. As we navigate the bicycles haphazardly propped near the entrance we talk about our choice for lunch. We're trying the Bacon and Peanut Butter sandwich with a side of fresh fruit salad.

The clatter of voices and biking shoes from the spandex costumed riders drowns out our conversation. Their shirts and shorts seem almost as colorful as the spring flowers blooming in the vineyard. It's good to see that business is up and the place is hopping given the sad state of the economy.

We are surprised to see the antique quilt as we head towards a table on the covered patio. Someone has decided to drape it over some shelving that is in the hallway that connects the two sections of the store. On our last visit in February, one of the clerks we quizzed hadn't really been able to give us a satisfying answer regarding the quilt's origin. We would just have to realize that the face we saw in the cloth was going to remain a mystery.

The breeze of the door opening from the patio lifts the quilt slightly as we step over to it revealing very tiny stitching on the back that at closer examination appears to be a date and a name, Mrs. S. Blaak, May 21st 1917. Now we are intrigued. All around us the collectibles and memorabilia from an earlier time would now certainly give us motivation to scour the barn for items of that era and through other times since then as well.

As usual the dusty old barn beckons, filled to the walls with treasures. While Jana looks for old milk bottles, I just stand in awe of collections of mirrors, old wooden window frames, and things of quality craftsmanship that have stood the test of time. What will our generation leave to the future I wonder? Anything like the quilt that now was piquing our imagination?

We end our time with tea, my senses thirsty for the subtle flavor of passionflower on ice. A pouch purchased to savor at home as well. We lift our cups in memory of Mrs. S. Blaak and her beautiful handiwork, thankful for our time at Jimtown and looking forward to our next visit.

SUMMER

'Tis moonlight, summer moonlight—
All soft and still and fair,
The solemn hour of midnight
Breathes sweet thoughts everywhere.
                    — **Emily Bronte**

As the Russian River Runs
by Simon Jeremiah

Coiling quietly out of Coyote Dam from

Lake Mendocino, the river runs south and west

Through the vineyards and gravel yards and campgrounds

Under the bridges of Ukiah, Hopland, Cloverdale;

By swerve of shore it makes an oxbow beyond Fitch

Mountain then returns over the summer dam at Del Rio

Woods and on passing Penelope's door (and sometimes

visiting her living room on darker days).

The river moves quietly today, its summer waters

Mostly underground and pumped up to the cities of the

Russian River Valley, to the grape fields, the swimming

    pools, the golf links,

Under the bridges at Wohler Creek, Summer Home Park,

Guerneville, Duncan Mills.

The waters gather all their forces carrying canoers,

fishermen, swimmers, kayaks, ducks,

flowing on, always moving until at last,

Weary of its wanderings, happy perhaps, it flows

Home to the sea.

Ballerina Skirts
by Chris Peasley

Yellow ballerina skirts
bob in the breeze.
A hummingbird flies
past an empty feeder.
It is the summer of
my entirety.
Quickly heading
toward autumn.
Summer now with
antique red roses and
pink geraniums.
Sweet are the crepe myrtle
blackberry and ice cream trucks.

I am frozen in the gaiety of the season,
red, white and blue stamps
the July yacht harbor
happy with colorful tides.
What part of my life
is taken with this
summer folly? I am
simmering in the heat
and listing toward shore's
autumn beat.
The maples are already changing.

Jimtown Store: August
by Mona Mechling

I AM NOW TAKEN TO HAVING DREAMS about the Jimtown Store quilt. There is something about it that makes me feel a kinship to Mrs. Blaak. Maybe it has to do with the resemblance to a smaller blanky version that was toted around by my toddler son all those many years ago. The design itself has no rhyme or reason although quilt expert Jana thinks it's a popular motif dating back to sometime in the late 1800s.

Driving through the valley with the vineyards in full leaf contrasting to the late summer suede hills, I am distracted by voices and laughter. Looking toward the river winding along the highway my eye catches the brightly colored kayaks and air mattresses with bathers beating the typical August heat.

Towering over the road are the oaks that I love so much, their ancient trunks with gnarled limbs reaching into the cloudless summer sky. I think of that living habitat, knowing what grew and thrived there was probably the inspiration of Mrs. Blaak at the quilting bees with her neighbors.

Arriving I see Jana in her sleek blue convertible looking sharp in contrast to the comfy old red pickup on permanent display in front of the store. The Jimtown destination is always a step back in time as the original store front has not been the victim of modernization.

Today we are feeling giddy and celebratory. We think some wine should go with lunch today to toast the launch of the *Vintage Voices* anthology. Another facet of our friendship is our passion for writing short stories in the hopes of publication. Hard work has paid off for each of us with this year's volume put out by Redwood Writers. Jana's story in the book is quilt-themed making this even more interesting.

Chilled asparagus soup is just the thing to go with a couple of glasses of sparkling white. We both spy the bread case and simultaneously point to the cheddar dill biscuit to accompany our lunch. Finding a table we glance about the store to check on the quilt. When it's not to be found, we decide not to waste any more time and begin consuming the delicious food. We'll wander to the barn afterwards, which seems to be where most of the antiques are stored, though why anyone would take the quilt out there seems odd.

The store is quiet and empty today. The absence of crowds allows us to linger more over the eclectic items found in abundance throughout. Jana picks up a teapot exclaiming, "I love this!" It will be the purchase of the day for her. I'm antsy to see the quilt and head out back. Mystery solved, I put my hand out for a pat to the delightful fabric. I tell myself that Mrs. Blaak and I are somehow kindred spirits, and I will know why before my next visit to Jimtown.

The Guest
by Chris Peasley

A fountain babbles incoherent
against carefully manicured
ornamental annuals
Demeter
Gentian, Pennyroyal,
mosses and fiery Impatiens

Cool shade envelops
tiled steps
espalier
Baby's breath
boy with lute
metal wrought
for beauty nothing else

In the distance
harsh sounds
betray brutish labor
dull eyes
mute
poverty's godchildren
inconsistent here

Silk sheets
Brandy decanters
parquetry
heavy towels
scented soaps
all for naught
but pleasure

Love at First Sight
by Armando Garcia-Dávila

"YOU DON'T HAVE TO TELL ME YOUR NAME," he says walking up to the bench where she sits waiting, "you fit the description to a tee."

She smiles broadly, "and so do you except that you are even more handsome than I had imagined." His grin displays teeth that are straight and white as piano ivories.

"Don't blow it," he thinks to himself. "Yeah, and you're more beautiful than I imagined."

"Why did you suggest the Healdsburg Plaza to meet?" she asks.

"Because it's where one should fall in love," he says. Her eyes flood with tears. Unable to control herself she rises, cups his cheeks in her hands and kisses him.

"My heart is beating so hard it's scary," he says.

"And so is mine," she replies. They extend their hands and weave their fingers together.

"Do you believe in love at first sight?" He asks barely able to keep his voice from quavering in his excitement.

"I suppose I do, but I fell more in love with you each time that we chatted online. Your being so handsome is only the icing on a delicious cake." Overcome by such a complement from the woman he has imagined sharing the rest of his life with, he stops in mid-stride whirls her around embraces then presses his lips to hers surprising even himself.

And she is a willing partner in a passionate and public outburst so unlike her normal shy self. She wraps her arms around his neck and kisses him drinking his very soul into hers. Fate is real, and fate is a wondrous gift that has come to her straight from the quiver of Eros.

She pulls her head back only long enough to whisper "I have never been more sure of myself in saying that I love you Kirk."

"What?" He says.

"I said that I, love, you, Kirk," she repeats with a smile.

"Kirk? Kirk who?"

"Kirk! Kirk Armstrong who loves snuggling by a winter fire. Kirk who loves walks on the beach, who loves an intelligent woman and cats, the same as me."

"I hate cats! I'll bet your name isn't Michelle who loves the Forty-niners, Budweiser and a night at the sports bar."

"Football is brutal; I hate it!"

"No you don't"

"Do so."

"Do not."

"And Budweiser? Budweiser? Paleese! Do I look like a bar-fly to you?"

"Next thing you know you're going to tell me you're one of those Merlot sipping wine snobs who sends money to public radio stations."

"I like Terry Gross!"

"And Oprah?"

"Even more!"

"Eat meat?"

"Vegetarian!"

It is said that to err is human but to really screw things up one needs a computer so who could have guessed that the two actually did wind up falling in love after such a rocky start. After their tempers cooled a little they decided that it would have been a waste of a Saturday night if they didn't at least try and get to know each other. By the time the night was over they had drunk a pitcher of beer (he drank all but a half glass of it) at the Healdsburg Bar and Grill. They shared a bottle of Cabernet with dinner in the Ravenous patio. It was dark by that time but the summer night was balmy and perfect for outdoor dining.

Two years later they married at Saint Paul's Episcopal Church to please Bob's family who required a church wedding. The wedding was soon followed by a seaside ceremony at the coast to satisfy Aurora's pagan beliefs.

He still hunts and she still volunteers at the pet hospital. Their little son was named Joe after Bob's father. His middle name is River after the Russian River; to satisfy Aurora's wishes.

They do love each other quite a bit. One has always secretly loved being around a male with primal tendencies; the other was secretly relieved that he didn't have to play the role of a super-macho quite so much.

Footnote:

A second couple, Norm and Norma had been e-mailing each other during the same time and managed to find each other on the same night in the Plaza on the opposite end of the same bench. The two shared the same likes and were also married but divorced after only a year citing irreconcilable differences.

Found Prose:
The ABC's of Requesting a Ride
(or perhaps why text messaging was invented)
by Margo van Veen

Y OU MAY HAVE HEARD about found poetry, but here is an example of its lesser-known sibling—found prose: The ABC's of Requesting a ride first heard on someone's answering machine. Only the title and division in four parts have been added, and for protection of privacy letters were used instead of proper names.

Part I. Introduction

Eh, good afternoon. This is B. and I'm in San Francisco, as you know. I just had a nice, long talk with C. and she is in a lot of physical pain, so—I had wanted to spend part of tomorrow with her, 'cause she had given me such a lovely birthday present last year, this time. Eh, this of course is my birthday today. Tomorrow I was hoping to go to Healdsburg and then jump on over to Petaluma for the rest of the Petaluma Poetry Walk, but now that's kind of up in the air since C. is not up to driving. So, I want to propose to you the possibility of your—eh—picking me up in Santa Rosa tomorrow at the Golden Gate Transit Depot, and our driving to Healdsburg together for the reading, and then may be popping on down to Petaluma afterwards, and then I would just take the bus home from Petaluma. Is that something that would interest you?

Part II. Snow job

Because I remember liking you and your energy and getting along with you as well as I get along with C. And she's not up to traveling right now. But we both thought of you as a way—as a way for me to get to both events. I normally wouldn't try to get to both events, but when I found out the Petaluma Poetry Walk was going to run late—'cause they've got half a dozen people who don't even start reading till six, I thought, well, may be I can go to both events—if you were thinking of doing that. And I don't know what your plans are; whether you are going to skip the Healdsburg reading and just do the Petaluma Poetry Walk all day—in which case I'd skip Healdsburg too, because I can always do Healdsburg another month (we both can)—or, whether we / I can do both of them on this birthday weekend with a little help from you. So, please, let me know how you think about that.

Part III. Disclaimer

And no matter what answer you give, it's okay. And I don't need you to feel obligated about it. But if… in order for me to work in both Healdsburg and Petaluma on the same day, I would need someone's help. X., who is my right-hand person, is going to be swamped with duties during the Petaluma Poetry Walk, so he won't be able to help other than to say hello and give me a hug when he sees me. So let me know.

Part IV. Summary

Again, the idea, the thought is for me to take Golden Gate to Santa Rosa and then to get a ride with you to Healdsburg. And then, if you either drop me off in Santa Rosa (if you're not going to Petaluma), or give me a ride to Petaluma and we'll both hang out there; and then from there I just get Golden Gate Transit home from Petaluma. So, let me know if any of that is of interest to you. And if not, well, I'll see you another time my friend. I'm at (415)--- ---- and my landline is (415) --- ----.

Ciao!

A Midsummer Night
by Dave Mechling

The long hot summer day
Winds down
The little river town
Settles on a lazy evening
A soothing breeze
Wafts about with the aroma
Of pizza and barbecue
The couple clink glasses
In a toast
While enjoying
Their meal alfresco
Music fills the air
A cool jazz plays
Beneath the band shell
A puckish towheaded toddler
Splashes playfully
In the fountain
Young lovers stroll about
Ice cream cones in hand
Nightfall overtakes dusk
Shops surrounding the plaza
Their windows aglow
With neon and the twinkle
Of electric candlelight
Invite us to linger
A little longer
In the moonlight serenade
Of the midsummer night
In the plaza

OVER
by Chris Peasley

The garden is filled with
a glory of roses.
Little pink single petals,
Large yellow frilled blossoms,
White roses like on a wedding cake.
And passionflowers and iris.
The scent in the garden is
heavenly, soft and delicate.
Many chairs in the garden
Adirondacks, wrought iron.
I sit in a webbed chair and ottoman
resting on the freshly cut lawn.
A small four-seater plane flies
overhead making a loud sound
from the prop engine.
I imagine flying over
this garden and noticing
all the wonderful colors
and me resting in the sun.

AUTUMN

Like a joy on the heart of a sorrow,
The sunset hangs on a cloud;
A golden storm of glittering sheaves,
Of fair and frail and fluttering leaves,
The wind blows in a cloud.

— Sarojini Naidu

Sonnet for Doug Stout
Who Sometimes Felt Like a Tree
by Margo van Veen

When I first learned the *Urgent News* of Stout
—this Douglas not a fir, though once an oak—
the poet's carpe diem message spoke
of baby seals too quickly grown, fleshed out.
Imagination's whale a blow full spout
or crude reminder all one day must croak?
Doug felt more like a willow than an oak,
memento mori on his mind no doubt.
A teacher, author, poet, playwright, sage…
whose musings on the future and the past
—fruit of experience more than of age—
include the pall by late-life's waning cast.
Now Doug is gone, but how his words engage!
this willow's gift to mortals, bound to last.

Autumn Farmers Market
by Chris Peasley

Lamb, chicken; out of goat,
cabbage, persimmons, Yucatan Tamales
wrapped in banana leaves,
hunting for summer sweetness digging
through a vat of tomatoes, unredeemed.

Pomegranates, gourds, purple vetch honey,
from sheep to rope and spinning wheel
from yarn to dye pot and hat

I wander and weave through
crowds looking for the perfect flower.
Fall is the best time to plant roses

> *in the garden*
> *my light shines*
> *apple garlic soup*

Jimtown Store: November
by Mona Mechling

I RUN STRAIGHT TO THE BARN. The quilt is going to be my personal gift, a tradition I always follow during my birthday month. Thanks to Jana's library of quilt books I knew the block was called Flying Geese. I had also come across an old newspaper clipping while in Google search about the Alexander Valley relating to the Blaak's, proprietors of one of the local businesses. It was an announcement about the departure of their son as he entered the US Navy and was about to ship out to WWI.

Trying to adjust my eyes to the dim lighting in the barn, I search for the quilt. Giving up after I realize it isn't there, I turn from the relics and catch something in the dusty shadow. I hear the quiet voice of a young man saying "Happy Birthday, Mom" and see the same face I had recalled seeing on the quilt back in February, but this time it was attached to what appears to be a lifelike form.

Mrs. Blaak and her son, in his WWI Naval dress blues, are standing in front of me in the shadows of the barn. Could I possibly be seeing a couple of smiling apparitions right in front of me? And as quickly as they had appeared, they are gone. Feeling a bit shaken I grope my way to the door and am relieved to be outside.

I am light headed from my encounter in the barn. I find my chair and settle into my seat at a table near the deli counter. Jana is there and I catch my breath, beginning to chatter about my experience. Her eyes grow huge in amazement. Although she wishes she had been early enough to witness the ghost in the barn with me, I feel that the apparition might have been for me alone to let me know that all is right with my own sailor and that he's safely on his way home.

It's two days before my birthday and I'm having a celebration lunch with my best friend and although I'm disappointed about the quilt, I am having an amazing day. This is the time of year I can't help but marvel at the beauty of the changing vineyards. The salad I have in front of me almost rivals the early November collage of colors outside in the valley. Red radicchio, the variegated greens of romaine all tossed together with purple onion and sprouts.

I am famished and don't hesitate to attack the plate with something more than petite bites. The taste of the pomegranate vinaigrette drizzled upon my lunch makes me want to lick the plate. I pop the remaining pomegranate seeds in my mouth and use my baguette slice to mop the bacon bits floating in the last of the dressing.

Our visits are not complete until we peruse the aisles as if we've never been here before, always discovering an item that we missed last time. The shelves are filled with toys and trinkets that one would find in a vintage mercantile. In the olden times not only would you go to Jimtown for your supplies, you'd catch up on all the latest news from your neighbors.

This store has been in existence since before the First World War. I pick salt water taffy and a few goofy things from a close by shelf or basket. These will go in the monthly care package that we send to my sailor son deployed somewhere in the Arabian Sea. I think of the young sailor from my barn sighting and wonder if the quilt was either a gift to be presented to him or a way for Mrs. Blaak to keep her mind off of war like other mothers in this millennium.

I glance up from my canvas shopping bag as Jana suggests a good-bye cup of tea at the counter. The pastoral view is worthy of a moment of repose. Jana orders fruity white tea while I find my usual comfort in Earl Grey. The steam curling from our mugs provides a tangible calming effect. My best friend's presence and the nostalgic environment of the Jimtown Store have put my soul back in sync with the earth and its gifts.

Epilogue: Arriving home from work on my birthday, along with the cards in the mailbox is a large brown package; a box from Jana...

Autumn in Saint Paul's
by Armando Garcia-Dávila

EXCEPT FOR THE MUFFLED RUMBLE of an occasional vehicle passing outside on East Street it is quiet in Saint Paul's Episcopal Church.

The walls and ceiling that are constructed of dark wood and the scent of incense hangs heavy in the air. Blood red, deep amber, forest green and blue stained glass windows cast solemn hues in this season of fading light.

An organ in the sacristy sits next to the altar, ten long pews to each side of the aisle and tall thick heavy candle sticks stand like sentries guarding the sanctuary.

Perhaps eighty worshipers could fit in this house of prayer. Been here a long time, this church dedicated to St. Paul. How many life cycles have been completed here? Baptisms for newborns, their weddings and finally their funerals.

The fourteen Stations of the Cross hang on the walls, seven to a side. The Stations of the Cross; a ceremony where a priest leads the congregation in prayer. He stops at each station that recounts the final hours of Christ's life from Pontius Pilate washing his hands of the condemned man to Jesus being laid in a tomb.

I never liked going to church when I was a kid but there was something about this service that intrigued me, a kind of morbid curiosity I suppose; hearing the tale of a man's slow torturous death.

I didn't ask him to die for me. If it was my sins that nailed him to the cross then so be it. I tire of feeling guilty because of my human frailties.

How many priests fresh from their studies at the seminary and eager to bring souls to the Lord began their ministry here? And for how many world weary pastors was St. Paul's their final assignment?

A chilly wind blowing from the north greets me as I exit this house of the God causing blood red leaves of a Liquid Amber tree to run down the street.

Healdsburg Morning: Autumn
by David Beckman

Ne'er saw I, never felt a calm so deep!
The river glideth at his own sweet will:
Dear God! the very houses seem asleep;
And all that mighty heart is lying still!
—from William Wordsworth's
"Composed on Westminster Bridge"

My heart awakens not to London or New York, not to Buenos Aires, Athens, Mexico City, Paris, New Orleans or Quito. But to a soft Healdsburg morning with the scent of dry leaves on the Plaza walkways, not yet raked.

I awake to the Russian River's slow westward sigh, seeking the Pacific on the far side of hills and vineyards. To the V of geese overhead, slanting down the morning sky with the purpose of a thrown javelin.

To the gathering Farmer's Market where, near Doug Stout's bench, a yellow van thinks it's a 15-foot-long outdoor planter with greenery vining from every window and door. I greet the driver and he greets me.

To the deserted asphalt lot of the burned and cleared post office where once love letters hunkered in cubbyholes like teenagers parked in a lover's lane.

To where North Street Craftsman houses nervously watch who's passing by as if it's 1944 and someone's not yet come back from war.

The pale green cottage at 325 First Street, whose front brick patio hosts a blanket of maple leaves curled like burnt paper and crisp as new money. And the cat two houses down armed tooth and claw and no doubt daring again to enter the lists against mouse and mole.

The driveway on Prince Street where a maroon Porsche 646 with a spoiler big enough to cook an elk on, dreams of turning fast laps at Infineon Raceway to the screams of pubescent girls.

The young jogger on Matheson Street, running as if to an important rendezvous, whose earphones thrum to the rhythms of Taylor Swift and Lady Gaga.

The chatter at the Goat where a couple's heads nearly touch above their table, and their words rise like coffee steam: *I would, would you? Yes, in a heartbeat. Where? Under a full moon.*

And finally, to the corner of Healdsburg Avenue and West Side Road and the paint-peeling Vine Street Gas Station, forever for sale, its rusting and padlocked accordion gates keeping everything out but cats and ghosts.

The Pain in Spain Is Hard to Ascertain
A Runaway Metaphor
by Margo van Veen

The pain in Spain is hard to ascertain
unless you get it.
This headline was inspired by a train,
but I don't get it.
> What is hard to ascertain?
> All the pain, all the pain
> But what ties all that pain
> to train and Spain?
The pain in Spain is hard to ascertain?
What's with this whimsy headline, pray explain?

> *These lyrics, though they rhyme*
> *neither fine nor sublime*
> *are in fact so asinine*
> *I'll deny they are mine.*

The metal steed of Healdsburg may derail
were we to let it.
No more literary laureates to hail.
Won't you regret it?
> People have you ever heard
> a poet run out of words
> by a mere figure of speech deterred
> concerning trains? How absurd.
The metal steed of Healdsburg may derail
its metaphors to some beyond the pale.

> *These lyrics, though they rhyme*
> *neither fine nor sublime*
> *are in fact so asinine*
> *I'll deny they are mine.*

For Healdsburg's Guild this clearly is a must:
Don't get railroaded.
But a private person's train of thought needs trust.
Don't overload it.
> What so clearly is a must?
> Faith and trust, faith and trust.
> Whoever keeps the train on track
> deserves a bust.

For Healdsburg's Guild this clearly is a must:
Keep local lit promotion the main thrust.

> *If these lyrics are a bore*
> *it's because never before*
> *has a simple metaphor*
> *about a train been milked more.*

The pain in Spain is hard to ascertain;
why let this headline run any longer?
But as the old saw says, 'no pain, no gain'.
What makes you suffer, may make you stronger.
> Now what was that cliché?
> There's no gain without pain
> Now the Guild is proud to say,
> Let's forget about Spain
Much better Healdsburg headlines can convey
there's room for all aboard the Letters train.

> *If these lyrics are a bore*
> *it's because never before*
> *has a train-based metaphor—*
> *mixed or not—been milked more.*

Let the metal steed of Healdsburg save the day
true to its purpose.
Support your local prose and poem train,
lit at your service its very purpose.
> All year long north of the Bay
> many stops you may make
> along the literary way
> make no mistake:
> *Don't forget to stop at Hopmonk*
> *and Word Temple for example*
> *or the Healdsburg Senior Center;*
> *there is haiku in Ukiah;*
> *the Poetry Walk in Petaluma;*
> *the Book Festival in Santa Rosa;*
> *slam events that need exploring;*
> *Graveside Readings never boring;*
> *open mics and featured speakers.*
> *Too many venues to be mentioned.*
> *Make no mistake:*
The metal train is bound to make your day
All aboard the local prose and poem train!

Flying Goat
by Chris Peasley

It's still early
skies still gray,
overcast and damp.
There are only
a few coffee drinkers,
scone eaters.
Two guys bogart
the newspapers
they probably didn't
bring.
A student with
earphones arresting
his participation,
studies a math
workbook.
I know because
of his calculator.
The paintings are
all landscapes and/or
impressionisms.
Oh well there was a point once
and then a child
comes in and takes over.
Priorities, yes.

A Quaker Man
by Waights Taylor Jr.

He listens attentively as I read him my lengthy manuscript, a
narrative history of the South in the twentieth century. Just
when it appears he might be asleep or dozing, he asks a
probing question that challenges and penetrates my meaning,
frequently forcing me to perform serious rewrites.

Who is this man?

His friends called him "Red," I called him Edwin. We were
both southern born and bred: he from North Carolina,
I from Alabama.

I came to know this man late in his life.

He was a redheaded man, this tall man called Red. He wore
the nickname like a badge of honor. I was also a redhead, but
I shunned the tag as if it was a badge of shame—too bashful
and too self-conscious to bear the obvious description of my
appearance.

World War II, a conscientious objector: defiled by most,
honored by a few. While others fought and killed in wars
in Europe and the Pacific, Red fought forest fires and planted
trees in Oregon, adhering to his Quaker roots and beliefs.

Europe, 1946: a Quaker volunteered to help rebuild the war-torn
continent. For one and a half years, he worked as a truck driver
and master mechanic in France, Germany, and Poland. He met
a lovely volunteer Quaker woman, Madeleine Yaude, and
returned home a happily married man.

I came to know this man late in his life.

Westward ho in '48; Red and Madeleine moved to Berkeley.
He unleashed his boundless energy, imagination, and Quaker
principles in the Bay Area for 25 years.

He developed the North Richmond Neighborhood House, a
social service and advocacy organization for the less fortunate.
He led this nationally known program for 18 years, while
earning a Master's Degree in social work at UC-Berkeley.

He and Madeleine started a shared-living community
of Quakers in Berkeley, where their two adopted biracial
children find companionship and acceptance.

The turbulent '60s; for six years, Red directed a Planned
Parenthood Center in the Bay Area that offered women family
planning and reproductive choices seldom before available.

Sonoma County, 1973; their children grown and on their
own, Red and others found one of the first community living
cooperatives in Sonoma County. Based on the Quaker
principles of seeking a peaceful and just world, Monan's Rill
sits on 400 beautiful acres in the hills east of Santa Rosa.
He was a founding member of Friends House, a Quaker
retirement community in Santa Rosa. In 1993, his beloved
wife Madeleine died, and part of Red died with her.

Red moved into Friends House in 1999, and the next year
he married Elsbeth Benton, a Santa Rosa Quaker. He later
told a friend, "I'm an incredibly fortunate man to have loved
and married two incredible, wonderful women."

I came to know this man late in his life.

Edwin is 91 when I meet him, almost blind, but still vibrant
and alert. I am 71, young enough to be his son or much
younger brother. He is eager for companionship, conversation,
and a reader. For once, I can satisfy all the needs of a single
individual.

In early 2010, he suffers a stroke that requires extensive care
and offensive treatments to stay alive. He said no, I won't live
this way, let me go. I visit him a week before he dies.
As I prepare to leave him, I take his hand and kiss his forehead,
and say, "Have a safe journey my dear friend." We both have
tears in our eyes.

I came to know and love this man late in his life.

He dies on February 17, 2010: a Quaker man, a peaceful man,
a loving man, a principled man, a visionary, a man of action
and courage.

Such a man was Edwin "Red" Stephenson.

Autumn Farmers Market
by Dave Mechling

Crisp air greets me
As I shuffle along the path
Leaving a trail in the leaves
That blanket the ground.
Early morning sun
Streaks its way through the trees
Where crows circle overhead
And call to one another.
The usually lively plaza is quiet,
To ready itself
For the up coming winter's slumber.
A grey squirrel is busy
Collecting its winter stash
And the bandshell sits quietly.

Making my way
To the other side of town
I turn my attention
To the day's farmers market.
Now that the bounty
Has been harvested
I am in awe
At the variety that remains.
There are jams and preserves
Enough for anyone's delight,
With apple butters, olive oils,
Even holiday wreaths and flowers.
Tables are stacked
With baskets of blackberries
Grapes and persimmons,
Peppers big and small
In red and green
Making me think of Christmas
All lined up
Under cover of tent like umbrellas.
Selling their goods
On tailgates and out of the backs of pickups
Like truck farmers of yesteryear.

Gorillas in the Mist
by Chris Peasley

They look like apes
rocking back and forth
in their baggy pants.
The predawn light,
the mist thick with
potential dripping from
live oaks and catalpa.

Their varied heads nod
in this fine spray
rising from the earth
and dribbling from the skies.

The bus stop holds
these creatures tethered
to this place until
transit comes to claim them.
Then they wobble onto
the Grumman with their passes.

Soon the skies will lighten
and the hoodies will fall away
showing the individual
natures of each mammal.
The red hair, blue eyes,
pin-stuck faces and tattoos.
Dawn will put out the
streetlights and gorillas
will melt in the mist.

Acknowledgments

FIRST AND FOREMOST, the Healdsburg Literary Guild and workshop participants are deeply grateful for the time, effort, and leadership Armando Garcia-Dávila brought to this project. Without Armando's enthusiasm and dedication, it is highly unlikely this book would have come to pass.

The beautiful cover, which likely first led your eyes to this book, was designed and prepared by Sharon Beckman, wife of workshop participant David Beckman. Thank you, Sharon.

The cover photograph was graciously provided by Barbara Bourne, a Healdsburg photographer. Barbara has a delightful studio at 14D Healdsburg Avenue.

Thanks go to workshop participant Waights Taylor Jr. for his time and effort in doing the layout work for the book you now read.

The workshops were held in Joan Samuelson's Healdsburg home. Joan opened her delightful home, only a short walk from the Plaza, with its lovely gardens designed to attract birds and butterflies to a group of aspiring writers. Thank you Joan for sharing your home with us.

Finally, a thank you must be extended to all the workshop participants. Without their interest and dedication in testing and improving their writing skills, this book would not exist.

Authors' Biographies

DAVID BECKMAN lives in Santa Rosa. His poems appear in *Present at the Creation*, the 2006 anthology of Sonoma County poets; in *From the Hills, Jackass Review, Blue Jew Yorker,* and *Western Friend.* His chapbook, *Times Three*, appeared in 2009. His latest chapbook, *Language Factory of the Mind*, was published by Finishing Line Press in December 2011. He's been featured at Healdsburg Literary Guild's Third Sunday Salon and Healdsburg's Literary Café; at Katherine Hastings's WordTemple Series (emerging poet), and at Ed Coletti's Poetry Azul.

ARMANDO GARCIA-DÁVILA has won awards for his prose and poetry and was named the Healdsburg Literary Laureate for 2002–2003. He refers to himself as the "Blue Collar Poet," and says, "I am neither an academic nor an intellectual and try to write in the voice of the common man." Armando also moonlights as "The Gourmet Poet," merging his loves for cooking and poetry by preparing first class meals for dinner parties and then reciting his poetry.

SIMON JEREMIAH lives on the right bank of the Russian River, where he keeps a small retreat for artists and writers. He is a founding member of the Healdsburg Literary Guild and remains active in the local arts community.

DAVID MECHLING has been writing for only a short time but has found his way into the local Sonoma County publications of *The Sitting Room* and the 2010 *Vintage Voices*. Watch for his collection of poetry and stories titled *Daveisms, miscellaneous ramblings from a suburban kind of guy.*

MONA MECHLING considers herself a "dark Erma Bombeck". As a teen, she began writing poems and short stories that went into a drawer. Her first story was published in the *Vintage Voices* anthology at age 50. Her writing is inspired by life in the 'burbs. Watch for her story collection, *The Fridge Magnet Chronicles,* coming soon to a bookstore near you.

CHRIS PEASLEY is a writer of poetry and prose living in Windsor. She has published one book titled *The Rows Between*, an entertaining book of poetry with art by her husband, Bill Geer. She is also included in a number of collections including *Present at the Creation* and *A Day in the Life of Healdsburg-2007.*

WAIGHTS TAYLOR JR. is a Santa Rosa writer. His first non-fiction book, *Alfons Mucha's Slav Epic*, was published in 2008. His second book, *Our Southern Home: Scottsboro to Montgomery to Birmingham—The Transformation of the South in the Twentieth Century*, was published in October 2011. Waights has just recently started writing poetry, short stories, and one-act plays. His first chapbook, *Literary Ramblings*, was published in 2010.

MARGO VAN VEEN lives in Santa Rosa. Her poems appear in *First Leaves*, the 2009 anthology of Bay Area writers, and in *Continent of Lights*, the 2010 anthology edited by David Madgalene, as well as on line at *Burning Bush*. She performs her poetry throughout the Bay Area and has been featured at Healdsburg Literary Guild's Third Sunday Salon and Ed Coletti's SoCoCo and Poetry Azul.

Healdsburg Literary Guild

THE HEALDSBURG LITERARY GUILD's mission is to enrich the cultural environment of the greater Healdsburg community through the literary arts. Our goals are to advocate and promote the literary arts by developing literary salons and other literary events that educate, entertain, and enliven our area. The Guild is a 501(c)(3) non-profit organization. Our Federal Tax ID number is 68-0315862, and donations are tax-deductible to the extent allowed by law.

The Guild has served the greater Healdsburg area as a literary venue for twelve years. In 2000, the Guild started hosting the monthly Third Sunday Salon in the City of Healdsburg City Council room. Currently, the Third Sunday Salon is held at the Healdsburg's Bean Affair—Coffee and More shop at 1270 Healdsburg Avenue from 2 to 4 p.m.

The Guild, with the support of individuals and literary groups in the community, has selected the Healdsburg Literary Laureate every two years since 2000. Current and past recipients of this literary honor include:

2000–2001 Doug Stout

2002–2003 Armando Garcia-Dávila

2004–2005 Penelope La Montagne

2006–2007 Chip Wendt

2008–2009 Vilma Ginzberg

2010–2011 Stefanie Freele

2012–2013 John Koetzner

Healdsburg Literary Guild
P. O. Box 1761
Healdsburg, CA 95448

www.hbglitguild.org

Made in the USA
Lexington, KY
21 January 2012